A13

DATE DUE

10-00   A/S

LA CAUSA

THE MIGRANT FARMWORKERS' STORY

LA CAUSA

THE MIGRANT FARMWORKERS' STORY

By Dana Catharine de Ruiz
and Richard Larios

Alex Haley, General Editor

Illustrations by Rudy Gutierrez

RSVP
RAINTREE
STECK-VAUGHN
PUBLISHERS
The Steck-Vaughn Company

Austin, Texas

Published by Steck-Vaughn Company.

Text, illustrations, and cover art copyright © 1993 by Dialogue Systems, Inc., 627 Broadway, New York, New York 10012. All rights reserved.

Cover art by Rudy Gutierrez

Printed in the United States of America
6 7 8 9 10 R 05 04 03 02 01 00 99

Library of Congress Cataloging-in-Publication Data

De Ruiz, Dana Catharine, 1945–
    La Causa: the migrant farmworkers story/by Dana Catharine de Ruiz and Richard Larios: illustrations by Rudy Gutierrez.
        p. cm.—(Stories of America)
    Summary: Describes the efforts in the 1960s of Cesar Chavez and Dolores Huerta to organize migrant workers in California into a union which became the United Farm Workers.
    ISBN 0-8114-7231-0.—ISBN 0-8114-8071-2 (pbk.)
    1. United Farm Workers—History—Juvenile literature.
2. Trade-unions—Migrant agricultural laborors—United States—History—Juvenile literature. 3. Chavez, Cesar, 1927–   —Juvenile literature. 4. Huerta, Dolores, 1930–   —Juvenile literature.
5. Trade-unions—Migrant agricultural laborers—United States—Officals and employees—Biography—Juvenile literature. [1. Chavez, Cesar, 1927– . 2. Huerta, Dolores, 1930– . 3.United Farm Workers—History. 4. Labor leaders. 5. Migrant labor. 6. Mexican Americans—Biography.] I. Larios, Richard, 1953– .
II. Gutierrez, Rudy, ill. III. Title. IV. Title:Causa. V. Series.
HD6515.A292U544   1993
331.88'13'0973—dc20   92-12806
                                                                     CIP
                                                                     AC

ISBN 0-8114-7231-0 (Hardcover)

ISBN 0-8114-8071-2 (Softcover)

To my sons, Mario Bernardo and Eduardo Felipe,
and to the children of Mexico and the United States.
(D.C. de R.)

For my mother, Helen, who found her way despite
five sons, and for my daughters, Kathy and Becky,
who helped me find mine.
(R.L.)

Introduction
by Alex Haley, General Editor

The story of David and Goliath is a familiar one. A young boy is called to fight a giant warrior. One is armed with a great sword, a powerful shield, and years of fighting experience. The other, the boy, is dressed in the clothes of a shepherd. He has no sword and probably couldn't lift one if he had. He has never fought in a battle. He does have a slingshot. He also has faith and courage—faith in the necessity of his being there to fight this battle, and the courage to act.

The story you are about to read is about a union of Davids. They are poor people, migrant farmworkers who harvest the food we eat as they move from place to place in search of work. They work hard and with dignity. They get paid very little and have nothing to make the job easier or more rewarding. They don't have real homes. Their children don't go to school regularly. They don't have much of anything. They are Davids who are so poor that they don't even have a slingshot. This is a story about how they find one.

Contents

1

Cheated!

It was the end of summer, 1940. Overhead, the California sun shone strong and hard on a young boy kneeling in the midst of a field of grapes. He was thirteen years old, and his name was Cesar. For more than eight hours he had been working under the burning sun. His back hurt from stooping to reach the fat bunches of grapes that hung low on the vines. Tiny insects buzzed around his face. He blinked to keep them out of his eyes and swatted them away from his nose and ears. His shirt was drenched with sweat. More than anything he wanted a drink of water.

Every day Cesar's sister, Rita, brought a large jug of water to the field. The jug was wrapped in a wet gunny-sack and left in the shade to keep it cool. It was water for the whole family—Mamá, Papá, Rita, Rookie, and Cesar. On such a long hot day, it was hard not to finish it too quickly.

This day the jug was already empty, the last drop drained an hour ago by the thirsty family of workers. There was no other drinking water in the fields. The man who owned the field was like all the other growers in the valley. Despite the hot sun and the backbreaking work, he felt no need to provide any water for his thirsty workers.

To get a drink, Cesar would have to walk to the distant farmhouse. The round trip would cost him almost an hour of work time. Cesar knew that his family needed every cent he could earn. He wouldn't get paid for the time it took him to go for a drink. It was better to stay thirsty and keep working. Cesar's workday might last another six hours—six more hours without water. But his family needed the money. Cesar kept working.

Cesar and his brother Richard, called Rookie, and their older sister Rita worked in the fields with their parents all day, every day. They worked Saturdays and most Sundays. For seven weeks now the Chavez family had been at this job, picking wine grapes. It was hard work made more difficult by the sharp-bladed Johnson grass that grew up around the vines. The Johnson grass grew so high it got in the way of the picking. In fact, this job was so bad that Cesar and his family were the only ones still working here.

A smooth-talking labor contractor had hired the family for the job. Labor contractors were paid by the growers and were in turn supposed to pay the workers they hired. But this contractor didn't pay them at the end of the day or at the end of the week. Instead, he gave them excuses. Sometimes he would hand Papá just enough money to buy food, which was just enough money to keep the family coming to work.

When Papá asked for the full amount, the contractor looked hurt and almost angry. He himself hadn't been paid by the winery, he would complain to Papá. His face would color with anger. Look, he'd say, this money is coming right out of my pocket. You should be grateful I'm such a nice guy.

Papá spoke only a little English, so he couldn't argue very well with the contractor. He took the little money the contractor gave him. The contractor told them they would be paid when the job was done.

The Chavez family had wanted Papá to quit after the first few weeks, but Papá said they couldn't. They had contracted to work seven weeks and they would. Besides, there was all that back pay they might lose if they quit. Maybe the grower would not pay the contractor if the Chavezes walked out on them.

The rest of the family voiced suspicions that the contractor had been paid already and was lying to Papá. Perhaps, said Papá, but when they were finished, the contractor would have no more excuses. So they kept working.

Now they were almost done. The next day was to be their last in this vineyard. They would work tomorrow, collect their pay, and be on their way.

That night Cesar and his family went back to the one-room shack they rented from the grower. Nights were lonely. There were no other children to play with. There was nothing but the low fields all around.

Waiting for dinner, Cesar and Rookie listened to the music of the crickets. They were glad to be leaving this farm and its long days of hard work. They were not used to being migrant farmworkers. They wanted to be back in Yuma, Arizona, on the farm where they had grown up. It had been their family's farm for years, started by their grandfather, Cesario Chavez, more than fifty years before. He had come from Mexico when Arizona was still a territory and homesteaded the land near Yuma. He built an adobe house and farmed the land, coaxing crops out of the dry earth with hard work.

Later, the land came to Cesar's father, Librado. Cesar, Rita, and Rookie helped their father work the land. They enjoyed helping with farm chores—feeding the animals, harnessing the horses. Sometimes they carried water in wooden buckets from the stream to the house. Sometimes they chopped wood for the cooking fire. There was no running water or electricity. But the smell of woodsmoke was a good smell, and the steam rising from the boiling pot meant that there would be hot water for bathing.

The two children remembered how different it was working in the high heat of summer back then. On their family farm, they woke up before sunrise. They began work very early, before the sun had a chance to get too hot. By 9:00 A.M. they would stop work in the fields, waiting for the heat of day to pass. Papá never made them work all day in the full heat of the sun, not the way they

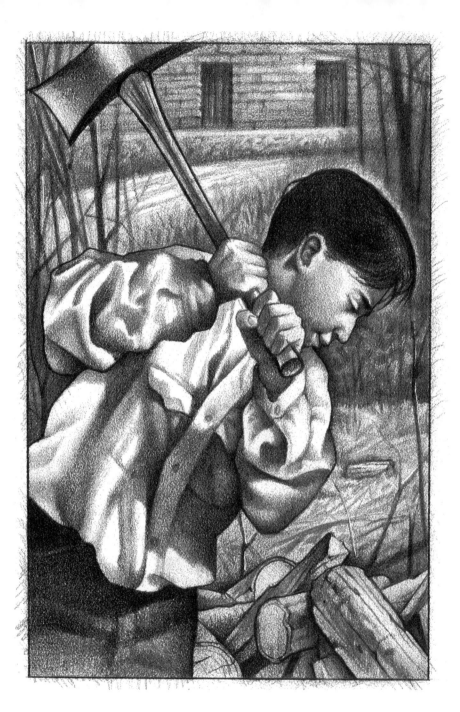

had to for the growers now. Working for Papá on their own farm had been good. Working for strangers who paid you little and worked you until you dropped was the worst.

The two boys were hungry. Dinner would be ready soon, but it wouldn't be much. When there is only a little money, there is only a little food. The boys remembered how in Yuma on summer nights like this one, the family would sometimes have barbecues. Cesar and Rookie could almost smell the aroma of roasting meat mixing with the smell of the woodsmoke. They could imagine the sizzle and spatter as the meat juices dripped onto the wood chips. Just thinking about it made the boys' stomachs ache.

It wasn't that the family was wealthy then, but they had enough to get by and enough to share. When people worked for the Chavez family to harvest the crops, they ate as well as the Chavezes. Wanderers, too, were fed. Mamá insisted on that. Even when there was only a little, they shared. "You always have to help the needy," said Mamá, "and God will help you." But now Cesar and Rookie felt *they* were the needy. And no one was helping them.

Earlier in the evening, Cesar and Rookie had

fished in a tiny brook near the shack. They had caught a carp. The carp gave off a strong fishy smell as it cooked. Everyone tried to eat some, even though it tasted of mud and every bite was full of bones. After all, this and a little rice was all they had after their long day of work. Tomorrow, though, they would have money.

That night, lying in the cramped space of the little shack, Cesar remembered lying under the stars back in Arizona. After everyone had eaten their fill of flavorful meat and beans, the stories would begin.

Cesar and Rookie had loved to hear stories of the Mexican Revolution. Some of the people who told these stories on the Yuma farm had actually lived through the Revolution. After all, it had happened not that long ago, in 1910. The boys were always thrilled to hear about the poor farmers and farmworkers, people like themselves, ordinary and hardworking, who had fought against wealthy tyrants for land of their own. Even now, in this tiny shack, they remembered the tales of Pancho Villa and Emiliano Zapata—especially the ones of Don Emiliano. He was the best! Many people tried to stop him and his armies of the poor. They tried everything to make him give up the fight, but he wouldn't, not even when they tried to bribe him. Don Emiliano would accept nothing for himself until he knew that all his countrymen would have land of their own.

Once, Cesar and Rookie had listened to these stories as they fell asleep on their own land. But these days everyone was too tired to tell stories at night. These days the family did not sleep as easily or as well. Pangs of hunger sometimes kept them awake, and the rickety cots in the shack were uncomfortable. Most important, the land they slept on was not their own.

It had been just over a year since Papá had lost his farm to the bank. His taxes were more than the money he made from his crops. When he went to the bank for a loan to pay his taxes, he was refused.

Just like that, the Chavez family had to move from their land, give it over to strangers who had never worked it or seen its crops come to harvest. Just like that, they were on the road to California looking for whatever work they could find.

Since then the family had traveled to many places and picked many kinds of crops. They were always on the move—moving to follow the crops. Tomorrow they would move again. The contractor—if he was not a crook—would come to pay them what he owed. That was what Papá hoped.

When their work was done the next afternoon, Papá had to go looking for the contractor, who hadn't come as he said he would. Papá looked, but the contractor was gone. No one knew where he was. And no one would pay Papá for all the work his family had done. They were told that every week the winery had paid the contractor for the Chavezes' work. It was up to the contractor to pay them. The people at the winery were sorry, but they claimed it wasn't their fault the contractor had lied to Mr. Chavez. It wasn't their fault he was a crook.

Papá had to tell Mamá and the children that there was no money. They had been cheated, and no one wanted to help or even seemed to care.

That night, the children slept in the car. Papá had no choice except to try to find more work somewhere, anywhere. Cesar fell asleep in the back seat, piled together with his brother and sister and all their belongings. He dreamed about the heroes of the Mexican Revolution. He dreamed about ordinary people who did what they could to make a better life for themselves.

2

You Work and Have Nothing

On a late afternoon in 1943, a young girl was sweeping the floor of her mother's hotel in Stockton, California. Her long silky black hair swayed back and forth as she worked the tall broom across the bare wood floor. Dust flew like butterflies before the broom. The young girl was small for her thirteen years, but she was strong. Every day after school, she and her two brothers helped their mother with the chores.

¡Dolores! ¡Ven acá! Come here! Mamá called. Dolores looked up from her sweeping. Several men stood in a tight little group by the doorway. Each held a box of strawberries in his hands. The men rented rooms from her mother. Looking at

their sad faces, Dolores guessed that they probably couldn't pay their rent this week. The berries
were being offered in place of the money they
didn't have.

Since World War II had started at the end of
1941, it had become harder and harder for local
farmworkers to find work. The government
allowed the growers to hire *braceros*—farmworkers from Mexico who were brought in buses to
farms and ranches in the United States.

The growers paid the *braceros* very little
money. They paid them so poorly that even if
local workers put in long hours at the *bracero*
rate, they were still unable to pay rent and buy
food for their families. Because things were
cheaper in Mexico, the *braceros* could get by on
the little they were paid to work in the United
States. It didn't matter to the growers that the
local workers couldn't live on such low wages. It
wasn't their fault, the growers said. It was just the
way things were.

Some local workers, like these men with the
strawberries, worked anyway. They didn't make
enough money to pay their rent. But they had
been allowed to take the berries that weren't good
enough to sell. They brought these berries to

Señora Alicia, Dolores's mother. It was all they could give for rent. Señora Alicia accepted the berries knowing that it was not enough, but that it was all the men had.

Dolores took the berries from her mother. The ripe sweet scent of the bruised berries was already filling the room. Later, she and Mamá would make jam out of these berries. Dolores liked lining the storeroom shelves with the bright glass jars of red fruit. She liked knowing that there would be plenty of jam in the days ahead.

As Dolores turned to carry the boxes of strawberries to the kitchen, she saw another farmworker approach the grilled window where her mother received the rent payments. This man was older, and he looked very sad.

¡Buenas tardes! Good afternoon! Mamá greeted him warmly as she wiped her hands on her apron.

Buenas tardes, Señora Alicia, the man responded weakly. Dolores paused, looking at his thin, tired, unshaven face. With one hand he reached up and removed his old felt hat, crushing it against his chest. With the other he presented a crumpled dollar bill—the week's rent. He turned away for a moment, as tears wound down his weathered cheeks.

¿Qué le pasa, Señor? What's the matter? asked Mamá.

"Ay, Señora, you work and you work, all day, all week. And at the end of the week you have nothing, nothing! You even have to pay for the ride out to the ranch."

Mamá nodded. Most of her renters were farmworkers. She heard many stories like this one. They always moved her to sadness, and the sadness deepened each time because the stories never changed. This poor man was proud and hardworking. Nothing could be worse than working as hard and as much as he did and still having nothing to show for it.

Dolores listened as her mother spoke with the man. Like her mother, she understood how exhausting farm work was. She remembered traveling to the beet fields of Wyoming and Nebraska with her father when she was four or five years old. They would stay in tarpaper shacks. No matter how long and hard Papá worked, there was still very little money. Every day they had oatmeal for breakfast; for lunch and supper they had rice, beans, and tortillas. On Saturday, there was soup.

Dolores's memories of those bleak days were sad. She went barefoot then because she had no shoes. Now things were better. She looked down at her saddle shoes and clean white bobby socks. She was proud of them.

A little over a year ago, her mother had taken over the hotel to help some friends. Mamá's friends were a Japanese-American family. When the war with Japan started, the government forced all Japanese Americans on the West Coast of the United States to give up their homes and businesses and move into internment camps. Most Japanese Americans lost everything. Some were lucky enough to have good friends who promised to look after things for them. That was what Mamá had agreed to do for her friends. Mamá would take care of the hotel for them until the government released them from the camps.

Now, Dolores and her brothers helped their mother do the work that kept the hotel going. They did laundry and ironing, swept floors, made beds, and helped however else they could. It was a lot of work, but Mamá needed their help. And they knew that after their chores they could go out with their friends or go to scout meetings, music lessons, or the movies.

During school vacations Dolores worked in the fruit-packing sheds. The money she made there helped make up for the renters who couldn't always pay Mamá with cash. It was painstaking work. For eight hours a day, she would stand at a table piled high with apricots. The apricots had to be sliced in half and laid in packed rows on a tray.

Using a small razor-sharp knife, Dolores carefully cut each apricot. She had to work fast because the more she sliced and packed, the more she was paid. Often, as she grew tired, the knife slipped, nicking her thumb and fingers. Her hands always ached from the work. They were sticky and stiff, and the cuts burned. Still, each day she worked until she had filled as many trays as she could. She was paid only a few pennies for each tray. A full day's work filled only six or eight trays.

Dolores understood how it felt to work long and hard for very little money. But she knew that her efforts at least helped her mother get ahead a little. The men with the strawberries and the tired, sad-faced farmworker with the crinkled dollar seemed to be working long and hard for nothing.

Still holding the boxes of strawberries in her hands, Dolores stared at the man. He looked like a prisoner behind the bars of the window. She knew he would keep working hard, and her heart ached to think that nothing would ever come of all his labor.

He was old now. Someday he would be too old to work. Then what would become of him? Would he be like the old people who sometimes went through the garbage cans looking for food? People who worked so hard deserved help. Why wasn't anyone helping them? Mamá always said that no one should be afraid to speak up for what was right. Why didn't anyone speak up for these people?

3

¡Viva La Causa!

Night was approaching. A woman in a simple plaid dress stood outside a theater in Fresno, California. She was small and slim with long black hair that made her look quite young. In fact, she looked more like a girl waiting to go to the movies than a leader of a new labor movement holding its first big meeting. But tonight would be full of surprises. It would be a night when dreams became real.

The woman was Dolores Huerta. It was September 30, 1962, and Dolores was now 33. She and her friend Cesar Chavez had rented this old movie theater for the evening. She and Cesar had met seven years ago when they worked together for the Community Service Organization. The CSO worked to solve community problems, to register voters, and to encourage people—all people—to take part in community activities. It was there that Dolores and Cesar first learned the skills that made this night possible.

Dolores entered the dark hall and breathed deeply. She was nervous, but that didn't matter. The theater's musty smell didn't matter either, nor the dust that settled like a gray snowfall on the old stage and neglected carpeting. Only one thing did matter: what the workers decided tonight.

She made a final inspection tour of the theater. Like her mother overseeing the hotel, Dolores was on the lookout for something forgotten or overlooked. But everything was in order. Nothing was missing. At the back of the theater was a table piled high with bologna sandwiches and sweaty green bottles of cola. There were card tables and metal folding chairs set up throughout the theater. Dolores hoped that enough people would come to fill every seat.

Soon the people began to file in. Their tired faces brightened with excitement and hope as they entered. Many had come directly from the fields. There were men in worn denims and dusty

20

workshoes and women with scarves tied around their hair. Children clung to their parents' hands or dashed ahead to find the best seats.

Dolores heard their many questions as they whispered excitedly among themselves. *¿Qué va a pasar? ¿Crees tú que puede servir esto? ¿Qué crees? Espero. . . .* What is going to happen? Do you think this can work? What do you think? I hope. . . .

Some who came into the hall had worked with Cesar and Dolores to help organize tonight's meeting. They nodded or exchanged smiles with Dolores as they passed. Some had tried and failed earlier to start a union of migrant farmworkers. They had been beaten or arrested or both. Tonight they wondered whether this effort would be any more successful than those of the past.

Dolores wondered, too. Would this idea of a union work, or was it too much of a dream? She walked through the growing crowd, working her way through the streams of people. Cesar had arrived and was on stage.

It was Cesar who had believed that the time was right to build a union. Others disagreed. Even Dolores wasn't sure, but Cesar had said to her, "The *only* way farmworkers will be helped is to start a union."

Dolores knew this as well as Cesar did. The defeated faces of the poor farmworkers at her mother's hotel still haunted her memory. From time to time at the CSO, she and Cesar had been asked to organize a committee of farmworkers to solve a particular problem. Sometimes they were successful, but often they weren't. They learned that more than small committees were needed. Cesar, in particular, wanted to work full-time organizing the farmworkers—not into committees, but into a union. Without a union, farmworkers couldn't get a fair wage from the growers. They couldn't get better working conditions or be protected from crooked labor contractors. They needed a union.

But the CSO always said to be patient. Everyone's problems could not be solved right away. Cesar, however, was tired of being patient. He didn't want to solve everyone's problems. He wanted to help the farmworkers solve theirs, and that wouldn't happen without a union. In March 1962, Cesar asked once more to be allowed to work full-time organizing farmworkers into a union, and once more he was told to wait. That was when Cesar quietly but firmly told the CSO, "I resign."

He asked Dolores to join him. But he told her she would have to quit her job first. She couldn't do it part-time. Dolores stared hard at Cesar. She wanted to know how on earth they would earn a living without jobs.

"You can't work for a living *and* fight," Cesar answered.

"How will we eat?" she demanded. Dolores had three children to feed. Cesar and his wife Helen had eight.

"I don't know," he said. "We'll eat something."

It was hard to tell who was crazier—Cesar for saying this or Dolores for believing it!

But Cesar had been right. Although their bank accounts emptied, friends and family helped them. Workers they talked to fed them. Cesar and Dolores didn't starve. They pressed on toward their goal.

There were many obstacles. For one thing, it was against the law to organize a union of farmworkers. For another, farmworkers were always on the move. They didn't work in the same place day in and day out, week in and week out, like factory workers. Most of them didn't even have home addresses to which union information could be mailed. But the greatest obstacle was simply that the workers were so poor. Where would they find the money for union dues? How could the union go on strike if it had no dues money saved up to buy food or medicine for its striking workers?

But Cesar knew all this. He didn't say a union was the easiest way; he said it was the only way. So what was the point in waiting? Why not get started now? Cesar could make the impossible seem practical. A union would work, he said, if the workers believed in it. Tonight they would learn whether the workers believed or not.

Dolores mounted the metal stairs to the stage. To the left was a sign that said, in Spanish and in English, "National Farm Workers Association." Using *Association* instead of *Union* was Cesar's idea. A farmworkers' union was against the law. An association—well, the law didn't say anything about that!

Cesar was standing on stage. He was very happy as he looked out over the growing crowd. He saw the hope and determination in their faces. These people believed. Cesar felt sure of that. He and Dolores greeted each other and settled in chairs on the stage with the other leaders.

Then a strong voice rang out over the crowded

hall. It was the voice of the singer Rosa Gloria. She was singing a *corrido*—a folk song—that she had written:

> *In the year '62*
> *with effort and uncertainty*
> *there began a campaign*
> *for the campesino.*
>
> *Cesar Chavez started it.*
> *He became a volunteer*
> *and went forth as a pilgrim*
> *to fulfill his destiny.*

This was the signal to begin the meeting. As the applause following Rosa's song died down, Cesar stood. Nearly covering the theater screen behind him was an enormous flag wrapped in brown paper. Cesar's cousin Manuel had made the flag for the new union. He and Cesar had planned it together.

As Manuel walked to the wrapped flag, a rustle of excitement moved through the hall. Some pointed. *¿Qué es eso?* they asked each other. What is that? Then Manuel pulled a cord, releasing the brown paper wrapping. People gasped. Cesar could see pride brightening their faces.

Cesar turned to look at the flag. In a white circle at the flag's center flew a black eagle, a symbol of strength and courage. Surrounding the white circle was a field of red. Red meant courage and union.

Most of the farmworkers were of Mexican descent. In the center of the Mexican flag is an eagle. And red and white are two of the colors in Mexico's flag. Cesar turned back to address the crowd. He described the flag as "a strong and beautiful sign of hope." He then introduced Manuel.

Manuel stepped forward. He explained that the black eagle stood for the strength that the farmworkers needed to face their problems. The white circle meant hope. The red background showed the workers' determination and unity in the struggle to achieve their goals.

Amid the cries of *¡Viva! ¡Viva La Causa!*—Long live the cause!—came foot-stomping, whistling, and applause. Into this roar of approval, Manuel cried out, "When the eagle flies, the problems of the farmworker will be solved."

Dolores and many others made speeches that night. All were received with great applause. It

soon became clear what the workers would decide. Sure enough, by the meeting's end, they voted Cesar Chavez president of the new union and Dolores Huerta vice president.

The union had begun. Now it was up to the eagle to fly.

4

Strike

Three years later, early on the morning of September 8, 1965, Cesar Chavez was sitting at his desk in the small National Farm Workers Association (NFWA) office in Delano, California. Suddenly, the door burst open and Manuel and Esther Uranday, friends and union members from the start, came rushing in with urgent news. The Filipinos were on strike.

Filipino Americans made up the second-largest group of farmworkers in California. They had their own young union, called the Agricultural Workers Organizing Committee (AWOC). AWOC had gone on strike for a good reason. The Delano growers were paying Delano's field workers less than they were paying workers at their other vineyards in the valley.

What AWOC did mattered to Cesar and the National Farm Workers Association. Cesar knew that the two unions would need to cooperate if they were to survive. If one went on strike, the other must also go on strike. Otherwise the growers could use one union against the other. But, Cesar wondered, was the NFWA ready for a strike?

For three years, the NFWA had been carefully building its strength. Dues had been collected regularly—as regularly as people could pay them. Even children offered to pay what they could, giving up candy or movie money if they had any. The treasury was growing slowly but surely. New union members were recruited. Needy migrant families received union help whether they were union members or not. Cesar had insisted on this. Others had asked why, with so little money, the NFWA should help those who didn't belong. Because, Cesar had answered, they are farmworkers. And when they see we can help, they'll join. Sooner or later, they'll join.

So the NFWA was getting stronger every day. But was it strong enough to strike? No one knew.

A strike could empty the treasury in a hurry. It could also break a union in a wink. People might give spare change and come to meetings. That was easy. They might talk over sandwiches and soft drinks as well. That was fun. But would they stay away from work long enough to win a strike? Would they walk the picket lines day in and day out?

"What are we going to do?" asked Esther Vranday.

It was a good question. Cesar didn't answer right away. He thought matters over. The decision wasn't up to just him and the other leaders. It was up to the whole union. "We can't call a strike," he said. "We have to take a vote."

Cesar was right. The union should decide this. A union run by its leaders wasn't much of a union, but one run by its members—*that* was a union.

In the meantime, he asked Dolores to visit the picket lines of the Filipino strikers. She was to work with the strike leaders and report back to Cesar. Within days she told Cesar that among the Filipino workers the strike was growing. Nearly two thousand workers were now on strike, she said. This was good news—great news even.

But there was also bad news. The growers had hired armed guards to patrol the fields. The growers said the guards had been hired only to protect their property. But the guards spent much of their time menacing the strikers. One guard had even shot at a striker.

A week later, on the night of Mexican Independence Day, a general meeting of the NFWA was called at Our Lady of Guadalupe Church in Delano. Just as on that night three years before, little was certain. Would people quit out of fear? Would the union take a stand? Would it stay strong and united on this question or break up into arguing groups?

First Dolores spoke. She told the union members in the packed hall about the Filipino strikers. She described how the strikers had been locked out of the camps they had lived in for years, and how guards patrolled the fields with shotguns. The growers, she said, want to slash the workers' pay by forty cents an hour. They want the workers to stoop and pick in the hot sun for one dollar an hour. One dollar. Who can feed a family with such a wage?

Dolores's report made the crowd angry. Everyone knew firsthand that this was how the growers were. If growers could pay their workers nothing and get away with it, they would. If not, they would pay them next to nothing. The Filipinos, Dolores told them, are on strike for a good reason, one we all understand. But they cannot win by themselves.

Her listeners shouted approval for the Filipino strikers. They continued to applaud and cheer as Dolores finished and others came and spoke. Then it was Cesar's turn. As he prepared to talk, shouts of *¡Viva La Causa!* echoed through the hall.

Cesar wanted to remind the union members of their Mexican roots and of the long struggle in Mexico for freedom. So he began: "One hundred and fifty-five years ago, in the state of Guanajuato, Mexico, a padre proclaimed the struggle for liberty. He was killed."

Cesar paused and looked at the crowd. He wanted everyone to know the risks. Those in the audience who remembered earlier attempts at forming a union or calling a strike nodded. They knew about the men with guns that growers often hired to "protect" the fields. Sometimes there was a scuffle or an "accident," and a striker was wounded or killed.

"But ten years later," Cesar continued, his voice rising, "Mexico won its independence. We are engaged in another struggle for the freedom and dignity which poverty denies us. But it must not be a violent struggle," he warned, "even if violence is used against us. Violence can only hurt our cause."

Cesar believed in nonviolence. His mother had often preached against violence when Cesar was growing up. He had listened and learned as a boy. As an adult he read stories about Mahatma Gandhi of India and about St. Francis. Both had used nonviolence with success, not just for themselves but for their causes. Gandhi had even used nonviolence to win independence for his country.

In the newspapers Cesar read about the work of Martin Luther King, Jr. For ten years, Dr. King had been leading successful marches and boycotts to help black people win civil rights in America. Dr. King's successes were further proof that nonviolence worked.

"The strike was begun," continued Cesar, "by the Filipinos, but it is not exclusively for them. Tonight we must decide if we are to join our fellow workers in this great labor struggle."

Cesar told the crowd that once they went out

on strike, they would have to stay out until their demands were met. It might take a long, long time. During that time, they wouldn't collect any wages. The union had some money to help the strikers, but not much. It might not be enough. Also, the growers might use violence against them. The strikers would need discipline. They would need courage. They would have to fight violence with nonviolence.

Cesar stared at the eager faces in the crowded church. Then he put the question to them. Would they agree to strike? Shouts of ¡Sí! echoed through the church. ¡Sí! Yes, the union would strike. They would join in support of the Filipino union.

5

On the Picket Lines

Two days later, in the quiet of the pre-dawn morning, Dolores Huerta pulled a long picket sign from the back seat of her tiny car. The air was cold and crisp. Moisture glistened on her old car's rumpled surfaces. The dark hid the car's bumps and bruises, its faded color and rusty edges.

Dolores made the short walk from where she was parked, by the public road, to a dirt track leading into the fields. Her footsteps crackled on the brittle ground. Nothing else in the lonely, empty countryside made a sound.

Dolores's fingers were already getting cold. She shifted the picket sign from one hand to the other. Her sign was hand-painted and held a one-word message: ¡*Huelga!* Strike!

She had driven for miles. Her eyes had searched the night for any hint of activity in the endless fields that covered the valley floor. But there had been none. Wherever grapes were being picked, the union wanted strikers. But with thousands of acres ripe for picking, the growers could start the picking anywhere they chose.

This was one of many points in the growers' favor. They knew the union didn't have enough members to send strikers to every field with ripe grapes. So the growers did their best to keep the union leaders guessing. They kept secret which fields they planned to have worked.

The union did everything it could to discover which fields were going to be picked. They had spies in the work crews. They sent cars of lone strikers out prowling the roads. This is what Dolores was doing this morning. She didn't know yet if she'd been lucky in her hunt or not. From the distant hills that made up the valley's eastern wall to the ground right by her feet was one vast inky darkness. The darkness made the fields as good as invisible.

Dolores shivered. At least she wouldn't have

long to wait. If the field was going to be picked this morning, workers would begin to arrive soon. They came between four and five o'clock in the morning. If no one came, Dolores would get back in her car and head for another field.

But now she must wait. She stood at the mouth of the dirt track, but she could go no farther. The track was a private road, belonging to the grower who owned the fields. If Dolores stepped onto that road, she would be on private property. She would be breaking the law and could be arrested.

The laws against trespassing were yet another edge that the growers had over the strikers. When other unions picketed, their members could walk right up to the front gate of a factory, office, or store—right up to where the workers came in. But striking farmworkers could not do this. Instead of one front gate, there were countless "gates," all over the valley. Any dirt road that led to the fields was a "gate."

And this field was too far away for picketing. Dolores could shout as long and as loudly as she wanted, but none of the workers would be able to hear her. If she took even one step onto that dirt track, the growers or their guards would appear like trolls and have her arrested as fast as she could shout *¡Huelga!* She would have to picket from here. Dolores began to walk back and forth along the roadside. She was picketing now just to keep warm.

After a while Dolores paused in her back-and-forth march. She planted her picket sign in the ground and leaned lightly on its top. As she paused, a rumbling noise, the growl of a car engine, broke the morning silence. Dolores turned. She saw the car, a big sedan, veer onto the shoulder of the road. The gritty, spitting sound of tires on dirt rang out. The car's snake-eyed headlights glared at her. The driver didn't steer his car back onto the road. He kept the car barreling down the roadside. He kept it aimed right at Dolores. And he didn't slow down.

The car's headlights burned brighter as the car hurtled closer. The roar of the oncoming car seemed to swallow the silence whole. Dolores was inside the roar, inside the blinding light, and the car was racing at her. She leapt back and fell to the ground, rolling away from the speeding car. It flashed by. A whirlwind of dirt and stones spun up in the car's wake, raining down on Dolores's sprawled form. She scrambled to her feet and ran to her car.

The sedan had braked to a skidding halt. The driver was shifting gears, putting the car in reverse. It shot backwards, its engine screaming. At the entrance to the dirt track it spun wildly before the driver calmly drove up the track.

Dolores, shaking, drove her car onto the road and back to the union office. Behind her on the roadside, her picket sign lay in pieces. Its handle had been snapped in two by the sedan's tires. The hand-painted sign was torn from the handle. The word *¡Huelga!* was still visible beneath the dirty tread marks.

Cesar Chavez had set up the union office as a kind of command post. Here, he expected to get reports on which fields were being picked and which weren't, so that he could reassign strikers. The reports he was hearing, though, were of a different sort. One striker after another began telling him of incidents similar to Dolores's close call.

An angry discussion about the union's tactics developed. Lone strikers were too vulnerable. They could too easily be attacked. If Dolores had been hit by that car, who would have helped her? Who would have been there to witness the driver's attack? *Nadie.* No one.

The union decided that from then on strikers would travel in small groups. No one would picket alone. Although this would help, it would just lessen the danger, not remove it.

The cowardly attacks on union members angered Cesar. He felt responsible for the strikers. But he knew that if the strike became violent, the growers would win. He reminded everyone that no matter what happened, there must be no violence by the strikers.

A few days later Dolores was again driving her little car. Crammed into it were picket signs, leaflets, and two young union members. The overcrowded car struggled along the licorice-colored valley roads. Dolores worried about her car. It was old, and she had driven it forever. The car groaned with age.

Dolores and her two friends were on their way to a field where workers were busy picking the ripe grapes. They were rushing to join the strikers already there when her car started to hiss. Steam rose from under the hood.

The car trembled, and then the engine abruptly quit. Dolores gave the steering wheel a shake of frustration before guiding the car to the side of the road. She had expected too much from her old car. For most of the day she had been on the road, driving here and there on union business. She knew if she drove the car too much, the engine would overheat. By midafternoon, under a baking California sun, that was exactly what had happened.

Dolores and her two friends got out to wait for the engine to cool. Once it did, they could replace the water that had boiled away and start the car again. But that would take time. Gnats buzzed up from the nearby fields and swarmed around the three stranded union workers.

Behind them the fields were empty. Despite long rows of ripe grapes, no workers were picking. There was no reason to picket here today. Or was there? Dolores looked up the road and spotted a house, the house of the grower who owned the fields. They could and would picket right here, just beyond the property line. Why not bring the struggle home to the grower? Dolores looked at the quiet house. She couldn't tell if anyone was home, but that didn't matter. If the grower wasn't home now, he'd find them there, picketing when he returned. Dolores told her two friends her decision.

One of the young workers pulled the picket signs from the car and handed them around.

Soon all three union members were walking along the roadside, picketing.

"Get outta here!"

The voice was loud and angry. Dolores looked toward the house. Her heart began to pound when she saw a tall man running furiously toward them, a rifle in his hands. He aimed the gun at Dolores and her two companions.

"Get outta here!" he said again. Rage colored his face and made his burly chest heave.

Dolores stood her ground, her eyes fixed on the man pointing the rifle. She would have to be very careful. She had no intention of backing down or showing any sign of fear—not if she could help it, anyway. But she did not want to make him any angrier than he already was. His finger was wrapped around the rifle's trigger.

"We're not criminals," Dolores said in as calm a voice as she could manage. "This isn't a war." The man just glared at her.

Cesar had said violence would have to be met with nonviolence. Dolores wouldn't back down. She couldn't. She told the man with the gun they couldn't go anywhere. Her car had overheated. They were stranded. She pointed to her car, its engine hood raised.

He answered by repeating his demand for

them to leave, a demand he now mixed with curses and threats. But Dolores didn't move.

On the wide, low valley floor, the two figures faced each other in an eerie silence. Passing drivers, astonished by the spectacle of a showdown between a small, unarmed woman and the tall, rifle-wielding grower, began pulling their cars over by the roadside.

Voices urging calm broke the silence. The grower refused to calm down. He threatened to start shooting if Dolores and her friends didn't leave and leave now.

One of the passers-by noticed the raised hood of Dolores's car. This seemed to give him an idea. He asked if her car had overheated. He asked the question casually, as if there wasn't a furious man standing there holding a rifle on Dolores.

Dolores nodded at the driver. He told her he had a jug of water in his trunk. Without taking her eyes off the angry grower, Dolores signaled to her two companions to go with the man. The three of them crossed the road and brought the water back.

While they worked on Dolores's car, the grower continued to mutter threats. But he no longer seemed ready to shoot.

When the car was ready, her friends called Dolores to come and try to start the engine. Carefully, she backed away from the grower and walked quickly to her car. She put the key in the ignition and worked the pedals on the floor. She held her breath. *Please start.* The little engine gave a raspy cough and gurgle. Then it turned over and caught. It was running.

Dolores quickly thanked the helpful man while her two friends jumped into the little car. Then, without a look back at the grower and his rifle, she drove away.

Maybe what she had told the man with the gun was wrong. Maybe this *was* a war.

6

If You Can

The pickers had worked through the long morning and into the early hours of the afternoon. The sun, even on this late October day, was hot. The pickers' weary eyes blinked constantly against the sun's rays and the relentless assault of gnats. Bandannas pulled up over their noses and hat brims pulled down low on their foreheads gave little protection.

Behind the pickers, hundreds of yards across the wide field, walked a small group of strikers. They had been waiting there in the early morning dark when the workers first arrived. At that time, they had called to the workers to join the strike. They were probably still calling even though the distance between the two groups was too great to carry the cries of *¡Huelga! ¡Huelga!*

For each hour of work in the sun, the pickers earned $1.20. It wasn't much, but it was more than the dollar they'd first been offered. And anything was better than nothing. They worked to feed their families. To strike was to starve.

The pickers had learned not to expect much more out of life than this. Join a union? What was the point? The union was small—most grape pickers had not joined. The strikers were sure to lose. Everyone knew that. Too bad, but that was the way things were. For now, the union was able to help its members by providing a little food or necessary medicine. But it wouldn't be able to do so for long. When it couldn't anymore, the strike would end and nothing would have been gained.

In the long run the growers would win *sin duda*, without a doubt. And then where would the farmworkers be? They would end up where they began—working when they could find work and earning what the growers felt like paying. It wasn't fair, but that was how it was. There was a saying that people had down in the barrio, the poor neighborhood, of Delano: *sal si puedes.*

Escape if you can. These workers knew that for most of them, there was no escape.

Suddenly, the afternoon's silence was interrupted by a noise in the sky. Some of the workers glanced up from the grapes they were picking. It was probably a crop duster on its way to spray a neighboring field, they thought. The drone grew louder as it neared. Instead of flying past, the airplane banked overhead and slipped down low over the fields. The right wing dipped and a scratchy voice bellowed out.

¡Huelga! ¡Huelga! it called.

Flying the plane was a Catholic priest. Shouting into a bullhorn from the open side door of the plane was another priest. A beaming Cesar Chavez sat behind the pilot. Cesar wanted the growers and the workers in the fields to know that this strike would not go away. This union would not break. It would be as pesky as the gnats in the fields. It would come every morning like the sun. It would find a way to win.

That was the way it had been in the first weeks of the strike. The union members surprised everyone with their determination and inventiveness. The nonstriking workers watched and they listened, and family by family they

joined. Union membership grew slowly, but it grew. Hundreds became thousands.

But the growers were just as determined to stop the union. They continued to harass the strikers. Picketing union members were insulted, threatened, chased, elbowed, and knocked down. They were sprayed with gravel by the spinning tires of growers' cars and trucks. Shotguns were fired over their heads.

The tactics of the growers, however, soon began to backfire. Despite all the harassment, the strikers didn't back down. They held their ground, and they held it without violence. Cesar had been right about the power of nonviolence. It brought sympathetic attention to the strike. Like the passers-by who witnessed the showdown between Dolores and the grower with the rifle, people saw the injustice and they responded.

What began as a trickle of support from outside the vineyards grew to a flow. Religious leaders were among the first to side with the union. Ministers, nuns, rabbis, and priests, like the two in the airplane, gave their support to *La Causa*. Civil rights workers came from the South, and college students from across the country joined with the strikers.

Outside support was important. It provided more people to walk more picket lines. And it brought hope to all farmworkers. They were beginning to see that this time things might be different. This time they were not alone.

Frustrated at the union's successes, the growers turned to a reliable old trick of theirs. They imported *braceros* from Mexico. After World War II ended, the *bracero* program was supposed to have been phased out. Instead, one "emergency" after another allowed it to continue. The growers always claimed there weren't enough workers to pick their crops. The government would then give permission for busloads of *braceros* to come north.

Cesar told the press that the *braceros* were scabs—strike breakers. "The poor of Mexico are being used against the poor of the United States," he declared angrily. Although its own rules said *braceros* couldn't be used as strike breakers, the government continued to approve their use by the growers.

Many of the *braceros* didn't know they were being used to break a strike. They were hired in Mexico and driven north on buses. As the big sand-coated buses drove into a grower's field, they would pass a knot of picketers holding signs. Someone in the bus would ask who those people were. The contractor hired by the growers would answer, Nobody. They're nobody.

If the buses unloaded near enough to the road, the picketers would call to the *braceros* in Spanish and tell them about the strike. Sometimes they would hand leaflets with union messages to the *braceros* through open windows as the buses drove by. Other times they would sneak with their messages into the camps where the *braceros* stayed. This was risky, but they tried anyway. If caught, they could be arrested or, worse, beaten by the grower's guards. Once Dolores asked her nine-year-old son to sneak union literature into a *bracero* camp. He was brave and quick and got safely in and out, leaving a pile of leaflets with the *braceros* before anyone spotted him.

Not all the scabs were *braceros*. Some were thugs hired to make trouble for the strikers. They would rip up leaflets, burn picket signs, and rough up union members. Reports by union members of violence usually went uninvestigated by the police. Union members, though, were arrested for trespassing if so much as their shadows crossed the grower's property line. Or they

54

would be arrested for "disturbing the peace" or on other "excuse" violations.

By December 1965, it was clear that picket lines alone could not win the strike. Cesar and the other NFWA members met to decide what else they might do. They knew they had to hit the growers in their bankbooks if they were to succeed. Strikes were meant to do that by stopping work. But even as more workers joined the strike, the growers found other workers to replace them. Something else was needed.

Once again Cesar looked to Gandhi and to the civil rights movement for an idea. If the NFWA couldn't stop the grapes from being picked, maybe it could stop them from being sold. The decision was made. The NFWA called for a nationwide boycott of grapes and grape products. Union members were dispatched across the country to ask people not to buy grapes or anything made from grapes.

At first the boycott did not go well. It drained union energies without causing the growers much concern. Then the NFWA realized that the boycott's aim was too broad. They needed to narrow their focus. They decided to choose only one grower as a target for the boycott.

They chose Schenley Industries, a company

that made many kinds of alcoholic beverages but also owned a few vineyards in the valley. This made Schenley a good target. The company didn't have much to gain by fighting the union—little of their profits came from the grape fields. But they had a lot to lose—millions of dollars in beverage sales. More than the other growers, Schenley could be hurt by the bad publicity the strike was causing. So the boycott worried Schenley, and Schenley's worrying in turn worried the other growers.

To work, however, the boycott would need time, publicity, and money. The strike was costing the union about $25,000 a month. The union needed money badly. Dues from new members helped. Contributions from new friends also helped. Cesar and Dolores raised extra money with speeches on college campuses and in town halls.

Other labor unions also lent support. Walter Reuther of the United Auto Workers visited Delano that December. He met with strike leaders and offered to talk on their behalf to local government leaders and to the growers. Both unions agreed to let Reuther speak for them.

When Reuther met with government officials

and growers, they listened politely but then told him that farmworkers were different from other workers. They didn't want to belong to a union. They were happy with things as they were. The people in the NFWA and AWOC were trouble-makers, not labor leaders.

Walter Reuther had heard this story before. He had heard it thirty years ago when the United Auto Workers was first getting started. And now here it was again. He looked at the hard faces of the men in the room and bluntly told them that they were wrong. "Look," he said, "sooner or later these guys are going to win. I can guarantee you that. Why not talk now and avoid all the bitter-ness?" But they refused. The farmworkers, they insisted, didn't want a union.

When the meeting ended, Reuther reported back to the leaders of the two unions. No one was surprised by the results—or lack of them. But before his visit was over, Walter Reuther did give the strikers some good news. He donated a check for $10,000 on behalf of the United Auto Workers to NFWA and AWOC. He had planned to give only $5,000, but as he addressed a cheering crowd of striking farmworkers, he decided to double his union's gift. The $10,000 was for the month of December. Every month after that the United Auto Workers would contribute another $5,000 to the strikers.

"This is not your strike," Reuther declared. "This is *our* strike! We will put the full support of organized labor behind your boycott." The farmworkers roared their approval. The NFWA and AWOC had a combined membership of only a few thousand people. With the UAW and other labor unions joining the boycott, a few thousand boycotters suddenly became tens of thousands.

"You are leading history," he told them. "And we march here together, fight here together, and we will win here together!"

7

Showdowns and Headlines

In February 1966, five months into the strike and two months after Reuther's visit, the situation remained deadlocked. The boycott had been going well, but Schenley officials, however much they worried, refused to back down. To win, the union had to find a way to apply more pressure.

Then one day a group of strikers picketing at a Schenley field was "accidentally" sprayed with poisonous chemicals. The strikers, coughing and gagging amid the moist cloud of pesticide, scattered in panic. Because the incident was made to look like an accident, no charges were brought against the growers. But for Cesar and Dolores this was one accident too many. They decided that the time had come to do something dramatic, something that would call the public's attention to the growers' tactics. Cesar came up with the idea of a protest march.

The march would be modeled after the civil rights marches that were going on in the American South and the religious marches, or pilgrimages, that were a popular part of Mexican culture. Union members would begin the march in Delano and walk some three hundred miles to Sacramento, the state capital. In Sacramento they would hold a rally, try to meet with the governor, and protest Schenley's actions during the strike. The march was to begin on March 17 and end twenty-five days later on Easter Sunday, April 10.

Preparations for the march were made all during February and into March. Dolores Huerta was to stay in Delano and keep the picket lines operating. Manuel Chavez, Cesar's cousin, would travel in advance of the marchers and prepare for their arrival in each town along the way. He would find places for the marchers to sleep and churches or halls where they could hold rallies to gain more support.

Cesar Chavez would lead the march. If all went as hoped, the march would make headlines

OREGON

CALIFORNIA

THE MARCH
TO
SACRAMENTO

SACRAMENTO

STOCKTON

SAN
FRANCISCO

OAKLAND

MODESTO

NEVADA

SIERRA NEVADA MOUNTAINS

SAN JOAQUIN VALLEY

COAST RANGES

MADERA

FRESNO

FARMERSVILLE

PACIFIC
OCEAN

TULARE

PORTERVILLE

DELANO

MOJAVE DESERT

LOS ANGELES

HUELGA

VIVA LA CAUSA

IMPERIAL
VALLEY

ARIZ

YUMA

ROUTE FOR
MARCH TO SACRAMENTO

MEXICO

across the country. People would read about the strike and the unfair conditions of the workers. They would learn about the boycott and maybe join it. Then wouldn't Schenley—and the other growers—squirm!

The day before the march was to begin, a group of United States senators came to Delano to hold hearings on the labor dispute. With them came television, radio, and newspaper reporters. The growers and local law officials weren't overly concerned. One of the senators was Senator George Murphy of California, a longtime friend of the growers. With his help the growers hoped to convince the nation that the strike was nothing but the work of a group of troublemakers.

But the union, too, had its friends among the senators. One of them was Senator Harrison Williams of New Jersey, who had brought the senators to Delano. He hoped the hearings would show that the farmworkers' cause was just.

The hearings were held in a high school auditorium on the steaming hot morning of March 16. A thousand people crowded into the auditorium to hear what would be said by the union, the growers, and the senators. They seated themselves in long, cramped rows of folding chairs.

Most of those attending were members of NFWA or AWOC. Picket signs rested beside the farmworkers' damp knees or danced in their thick hands as they demonstrated their support for the strike. Outside, several hundred more people waited for news from the hearings.

Inside the auditorium, sweating people fanned themselves with folded scraps of paper and waited for the hearing to start. Tomorrow, some of these spectators would begin the march to Sacramento. But today everyone's attention was on the senators. Anxiously, the crowd watched the table where the senators and their aides were gathering. What would be said? Would the senators understand?

At last the hearings began. The growers tried to convince the senators that the strike was the work of "outside agitators"—professional troublemakers who had come to Delano to stir up otherwise content people. No one but these troublemakers wanted a union, the growers claimed. Get rid of the outside agitators, and there would be no strike.

But even with Senator Murphy's help, the growers couldn't persuade the other senators or the reporters covering the hearings that all the

63

people in the auditorium were "outside agitators." Their callused hands and sun-creased faces made it clear that they were farmworkers. Their signs and NFWA or AWOC buttons identified them as union members.

And when Cesar Chavez testified, there was no doubt that he, a farmworker from Delano, was their leader.

Cesar told the senators that the farmworkers' problems were old ones. There had been hearings before about their difficult life—the long hours, the horrible conditions, the low pay. "Although we appreciate your efforts here," he told the hearing, "we do not believe that public hearings are the route to solving the problem of the farmworker. In fact, I do not think that anyone should ever hold another hearing or make a special investigation of the farm labor problem."

There was silence behind Cesar as he spoke. His black hair hung forward as he leaned toward the microphone. Perspiration beaded his forehead. "Everything has been recorded too many times already," he added with obvious frustration.

Cesar said that some people were telling farmworkers they should be patient. Such people were saying that education would solve the problem, not for the farmworkers, Cesar pointed out, but for their children. "Write off this generation of parents, and hope my son gets out of farm work" was how Cesar described the argument.

"Well, I am not ready to be written off as a loss," he declared. "And farm work could be a decent job for my son *with* a union. All we want from the government is the recognition of our right to full and equal coverage under every law which protects every other working man and woman in this country. What we demand is very simple. We want equality."

Cesar's remarks had a particular impact on Senator Robert Kennedy of New York. Senator Kennedy admired the frankness of Cesar's testimony. It went a long way toward convincing the senator that the farmworkers were right to demand better treatment from the growers.

A few minutes later, the testimony of one of the growers' best friends, Sheriff Leroy Galyen, further convinced the senator that the farmworkers' cause was a fight for justice. Sheriff Galyen described an event that had occurred a short time before the senators arrived in Delano. More than twenty strikers had been arrested by the sheriff while they picketed a field being worked by scabs.

Senator Kennedy asked why the strikers had been arrested.

"Well," said the sheriff, "if I have reason to believe that there's going to be a riot started, and somebody tells me that there's going to be trouble if you don't stop them, it's my duty to stop them."

"And who told you that they were going to riot?" asked Senator Kennedy.

The sheriff replied that some of the scabs had come to talk to him. "The men . . . said, 'If you don't get them out of here, we're going to cut their hearts out.' So rather than let them get cut, we removed the cause."

Kennedy, who had been the U.S. Attorney General before becoming a senator, was dumbfounded. American citizens who were peacefully and lawfully exercising their rights were threatened with violence by another group right before the eyes of an officer of the law. Yet this officer had then ordered the arrest of the threatened *victims* as the "cause" of the trouble.

"This is the most interesting concept," Senator Kennedy commented drily. "How can you arrest somebody if they haven't violated the law?"

"They were ready to violate the law," the sheriff answered. He added that the local district attorney had supported his action.

Senator Murphy commended the sheriff for his concern for public safety. Then he moved that the hearing break for lunch.

But Senator Kennedy cut in. "Can I suggest," he said sharply, "that in the interim period of time, the luncheon period of time, that the sheriff and the district attorney read the Constitution of the United States?"

The senators left that afternoon, but reporters stayed to write about the hearings. Their stories recounted the testimony of Cesar Chavez, told of Kennedy's support of a farmworkers' union, and described the showdown between the senator and the sheriff. The hearings didn't resolve anything, but they made headlines in California and were reported all over the country.

The next morning another showdown occurred, this one between the marchers and Police Chief James Ailes. The marchers had been given permission to begin their march on Albany Street, located on the outskirts of town. But when the 67 marchers assembled at the Delano office of NFWA, Cesar changed his mind. If they marched down Albany, few people would see them.

Instead, he decided, they would march right through the center of town.

Chief Ailes was furious. He made up his mind to stop the march before it even got started. He and his police officers quickly blocked the path of the marchers and ordered them to disband. You don't have a permit for this march, he told them.

The marchers stopped, but they didn't disband. Some began to kneel. They would pray, but they would not leave. Chief Ailes was about to arrest every marcher who refused to move when he noticed the gathering reporters, still in Delano from the day before.

He hesitated. It wouldn't look good for the city of Delano if he began arresting people in front of all these news people.

The hot sun beat down on the line of marchers, who were patiently standing or kneeling in place. Reporters and photographers waited in anticipation of a big story. Chief Ailes was joined by the Delano city manager. The two men had a hurried conversation.

Cesar remained at the head of the line with his father. Librado Chavez was now over eighty years old. He had waited all his life for the chance to stand up for himself and others like him. Like his son, he was willing to walk all day or wait all day or go to jail. Whatever it took to spread the word of the *huelga*, he was ready to do. Like his son, he refused to allow himself to be written off as a loss.

In the still air, flags hung limply from their poles. Police radios buzzed and crackled in the cars blocking the path of the marchers. Blue-uniformed officers stood waiting for orders.

Chief Ailes was no fool. He knew that to arrest the marchers would make headlines all over the country. He would have to swallow his anger. He and the city manager decided to let the march pass through the center of town.

The road was cleared. The marchers stood tall, their faces filled with determination and hope. The long march to Sacramento began.

8

The Road to Sacramento

With their small victory on the streets of Delano fresh in their minds, the 67 marchers headed north through the valley. Many of them carried colorful symbols: the American flag, the Mexican and Filipino flags, the *huelga* flag with its black eagle, and the banner of Our Lady of Guadalupe. Some marchers wore hats with red hatbands displaying the black eagle. Others wore armbands showing the black eagle's wings spread against a red background.

The NFWA had chosen the 67 marchers carefully. The union wanted the heart of the march to be a group who could walk the whole three hundred miles. Hundreds had volunteered, but union doctors had rejected those in poor health or those, like Cesar's father Librado, who seemed too weak or old to make the entire journey. Still, many of those rejected walked some distance with the marchers to show their support before returning home.

People who watched the line of marchers pass reacted in different ways. Some shouted insults or made threatening gestures. Others were friendly and waved to the marchers. On one stretch of the road out of Delano, the march filed past growers' homes. Some of the homes had tables set up in the front yards. Various products made by Schenley Industries were displayed on these tables, along with signs that read *In this house we use Schenley products.*

This early part of the march was deep in strike territory. The marchers had been told to be prepared for hostile words and other opposition. But other than an occasional angry shout, there was no trouble.

By the end of the first day, the marchers had covered about 21 miles. They were tired and sore, and many had blistered feet.

Among those in the worst condition was Cesar himself. His back had been hurting even before the march began. To make matters worse, he hadn't had time to buy a pair of sturdy boots. Instead, he wore old shoes. He walked with an uneven stride, favoring his right leg. Before long, his left foot began to hurt. Just eight miles into the march, the sole of Cesar's foot was covered with blisters. By evening he was in agony.

A woman who lived in a tiny cabin offered the marchers the use of her home for the night. Some of the marchers slept in her cabin. Others spent the night outside on the lawn. Peggy McGivern, an NFWA nurse, tended to sore feet, blistered heels, and insect bites. She soaked Cesar's throbbing foot in water, but he refused to take painkillers.

The marchers traveled 17 miles the next day, 12 miles more the day after. By the end of the third day, Cesar's left leg was swollen all the way up to his thigh. A fever drenched him in sweat. Still he insisted on walking with the marchers. Finally, his fever rose so high that Peggy McGivern pulled him from the line and put him in her station wagon.

Cesar did not stay out of the march for long. Less than a day later, he was back on his feet. Someone gave him a cane, and this seemed to help. His fever broke that night, and, in the days that followed, his strength gradually returned.

The farther the marchers traveled, the more notice they attracted. Although some people yelled threats and insults, much of the attention was friendly and even helpful. As the marchers passed through towns and cities, they were often greeted by people handing out sandwiches, cans of soft drinks, and whatever else they could spare.

One day, the group passed a small shack. Cesar watched in amazement as a family came out of the shack and hurried toward the marching line. Family members were carrying glass cups and a bowl filled with punch. The teenaged daughters ran down the line of marchers, handing out cups of punch. The cool drink quenched Cesar's thirst, but the generosity of this family refreshed him even more.

The marchers continued on toward Sacramento, tired but determined. In each town they passed through, more supporters greeted them and urged them on. Waves and shouts of encouragement were coming now not just from other farmworkers and union members, but also from high school and college students, teachers, and religious leaders. Other people, too—from bank tellers and writers to folk singers and movie stars—added their support.

Many of these supporters joined the march, walking side by side with the farmworkers. As the marchers moved on, Cesar and the others could still hear some people yelling insults. But now the voices of those in favor of *La Causa* had grown far louder than those against. And for every person who joined the march, there were dozens, perhaps hundreds, who joined the boycott against Schenley products.

After nine days the group reached Fresno, almost a third of the way to the capital. With the help of the cane, Cesar was walking with much less pain. Since the group was ahead of schedule, they slowed to a less punishing pace. Fresno Mayor Floyd Hyde gave the marchers a luncheon. Hundreds of Fresno's citizens joined the march through their city.

Cesar felt wonderful to be in an entire city of supporters. Even better was the knowledge that the publicity from the march was drawing more and more attention to the boycott. Perhaps the march in itself would not cause Schenley to give in to the farmworkers' union. But a truly effective and widespread boycott of Schenley products might do just that.

On March 31, Cesar's birthday, the marchers reached Modesto. Cesar knew that the support for *La Causa* had now grown to a point where it must be making Schenley officials increasingly uneasy. As he walked through Modesto, he saw that the nation's largest labor union, the AFL-CIO, had lined the streets with representatives of dozens of local unions. Cesar saw electricians, carpenters, painters, bricklayers, and other laborers standing along his route with signs identifying their unions and declaring their support. The signs read *Viva La Causa* and *Viva La Huelga*.

That evening in Modesto the marchers celebrated both the mounting success of the march and Cesar Chavez's birthday. Everyone was feeling very festive.

Two days later, the march reached Stockton. There, the greeting from supporters was even greater than the marchers had hoped. Thousands of men, women, and children blocked the streets, their cheers growing louder as the line of marchers approached. People waved and threw flowers while mariachi bands played Mexican songs. The crowds were so thick that it took the marchers over two hours to walk less than four miles. But the best was yet to come.

That night Cesar was getting ready for an evening rally at a nearby park. He was filled with excitement but very tired. An aide came by to say that there was a telephone call for him. Cesar was in a hurry so he asked the aide to take a message. A moment later the aide returned. "The guy said that he wants to talk to you because he wants to sign a contract. He says he's from Schenley."

Cesar thought for a second, then told the aide to hang up. "I've heard that story before," Cesar said. He and Dolores Huerta and anyone else who worked at the union office got all too many such prank calls. Callers would promise settlements, then burst into laughter and hang up. Cesar was too busy to waste his time on practical jokers.

Five minutes later the aide returned once more. The man had called back. "Cesar, he's got to talk to you."

Cesar stormed over to the phone and grabbed the receiver. He heard a man's voice say, "I want to talk to you about recognizing the union and signing a contract."

"Oh, yeah," said Cesar. "What else is new?" And he hung up the phone angrily.

But before Cesar could walk away, the phone

was ringing again. *"Look,"* said the caller urgently, *"I'm serious!"*

And he was. His name was Sidney Korshak, and he was a lawyer hired to represent Schenley Industries. Korshak wanted Cesar to meet him the next morning in Beverly Hills, a suburb of Los Angeles.

Cesar spent the rest of the evening on the telephone. He called Manuel Chavez, Dolores Huerta, and other NFWA leaders. He called the leaders of AWOC, too. He needed permission from everyone before he could negotiate a contract with Schenley.

Finally, hours later, Cesar prepared to leave Stockton. Union members called after him with best wishes and with more advice and reminders than any one person could remember.

It was 1:00 A.M. when Cesar's car drove off. The trip south to Beverly Hills would take over six hours. A friend drove while Cesar slept in the back seat.

Many years before, Cesar had slept in the back seat of his father's car. His parents had lost their home, and they were on their way from one bad job to another. They needed help, but there was no one to give it. Cesar was just a little boy then, sleeping in a pile of children as the car jolted along country roads. On that night long ago, he had dreamed about heroes: people who helped others improve their lives. Tonight, heading for Beverly Hills, he was about to become just such a hero.

The next morning, Cesar Chavez negotiated a contract with representatives from Schenley Industries. The contract recognized the farmworkers' union and gave the workers the raise they'd asked for. It also provided for a hiring hall, so that the union, not dishonest contractors, would match workers with available jobs. The contract also supported a credit union for the NFWA, which would enable members to borrow money at special low rates. All in all, not a bad morning's work!

Cesar rejoined the march, bringing with him news of the union's first big victory. A few days later, on Easter Sunday, the marchers reached Sacramento, where a huge, cheering crowd made them forget all about their tired legs and aching feet. An estimated eight thousand to ten thousand people rallied in welcome and support, jamming the area around the capitol building.

The NFWA eagle was soaring. It flew on flags

of red, white, and black, on bedsheet banners, and on cardboard signs. The eagle proclaimed its message of courage, unity, and hope. At long last, the union was on its way.

Epilogue

For the farmworkers, the Schenley contract was like the Battle of Lexington and Concord in the American Revolution. It was their shot heard round the world. And it was only the beginning.

Immediately after the Schenley contract was signed, the union targeted the Di Giorgio Corporation, the biggest grape grower in the Delano region. After several difficult months, the farmworkers won their second victory. During the struggle with Di Giorgio, NFWA and AWOC merged into the United Farm Workers Organizing Committee (UFWOC). The United Farm Workers then fought a five-year battle with the largest growers in the state of California. The union won that difficult struggle as well.

Since then there have been more victories. None have come easily. Many more are still needed before the dreams of equality that Cesar Chavez and Dolores Huerta share with the migrant farmworkers are realized. Today the United Farm Workers work as tirelessly and as relentlessly for the rights and dignity of the workers as Chavez and his friends did in the years of the union's birth. And, just as it did on the day of their first victory, the eagle is still flying.

Afterword

The authors would like to thank Dolores Huerta and Esther Uranday for their help in the preparation of this manuscript. We are also indebted to the fine work of other writers in recording the history of La Causa. Particularly helpful were Jacques Levy's *Cesar Chavez, Autobiography of La Causa;* John Gregory Dunne's *Delano, The Story of the California Grape Strike;* Dick Meister and Anne Loftis's *A Long Time Coming, The Struggle to Unionize America's Farm Workers;* and Peter Matthiessen's *Sal Si Puedes, Cesar Chavez and the New American Revolution.*

All the conversations that were presented in the story in quotation marks are the exact words used by the people involved. They were either recorded at the time of the events of the story, or were remembered by the participants in later accounts. Those not presented in quotations are summaries or paraphrases of people's words or thoughts.

Some narrative details—the shine of morning dew on a car fender or the sound of tires on a dirt road— were added where our sources did not provide them. But all the events and characters are real, the story true.

Notes

Page 5   Cesario Chavez, Cesar's grandfather, had known injustice in Mexico as well. There he had worked as a field laborer for a wealthy rancher who kept workers bound to him by debt. The rancher even maintained an account of what it cost to feed a worker's baby from the day it was born. By the time that child was old enough to work, he was already heavily in debt to the rancher. In the 1880s, Cesario Chavez escaped the ranch in the middle of the night and crossed into Texas. He was able to homestead his own land in the Arizona Territory soon afterward.

Pages 8–9   The Mexican Revolution came about after years of dictatorship by Porfirio Diaz (1830–1915), who had ruled Mexico for most of the years since 1876. Under his rule, most of the land was owned by the rich. Their huge estates were worked by farm laborers like Cesario Chavez, who were treated as little better than slaves. Factory workers did not do much better: They were paid low wages and were not allowed to form labor unions. Liberal leaders finally tried to overthrow the Diaz government by force of arms. Bands of revolutionaries formed all over Mexico. Among the leaders of the revolution were Pancho Villa (1871–1923) and Emiliano Zapata (1879–1919). It was Zapata especially who wanted the revolution to lead to land reform, so that poor peasants could own their own land.

Page 9   Librado Chavez was one of many who lost farms, businesses, and even homes because they were unable to pay off taxes or mortgages during the Depression years of the 1930s. Although the state of Arizona took possession of the farm in 1937, the law allowed Librado Chavez time to try to raise the money needed to save the farm. At that point, he went to California alone as a seasonal farm worker. Then he brought his family to join him in the fields. But even their combined wages were far too low to earn the money they needed. The farm was sold off in 1939, and the Chavez family took to the road for good.

Page 12   Although World War II actually began in September 1939, when Germany attacked Poland, the United States at first tried to stay out of the war. Then on December 7, 1941, Japan attacked Hawaii, which was a United States territory at the time. The United States then declared war against Japan. A few days later Germany and Italy, Japan's allies, declared war against the United States.

Page 16   In February 1942, President Franklin Roosevelt signed Executive Order 9066. This order allowed the War Department to call any area on the

West Coast a military zone. The order was designed to remove Japanese Americans from the coastal areas. Anti-Japanese sentiment, fueled by racism and war fever, was responsible for this injustice. With absolutely no evidence to support the action, the government declared an entire race of Americans a "security risk." More than 110,000 people of Japanese ancestry, most of whom were American citizens, including some U.S. veterans of World War I, were forced into concentration camps farther inland.

Page 20 The Community Service Organization (CSO) began among unskilled workers in the Mexican-American *barrio,* or neighborhood, of East Los Angeles in the mid-1940s. One CSO effort was conducting voter-registration drives. The CSO also called for investigations of the way in which voter registration was conducted in California. As with African Americans of those days who tried to vote, Mexican Americans were often forced to pass literacy tests in order to register to vote. Many thus became discouraged and stayed away from the polls. One man active in organizing local CSO chapters was Fred Ross. It was Ross who first brought both Cesar Chavez and Dolores Huerta into the CSO—Chavez in 1952, and Huerta three years later.

Page 35 St. Francis of Assisi (1181?–1226) gave up

all claim to his family's wealth to live a life of poverty, dedicating himself to caring for the poor and the sick. Mohandas Gandhi (1869–1948), called *Mahatma* or "great soul," was a social reformer who helped India gain independence from Great Britain. He developed effective methods of nonviolent resistance that could be used by even the poor and powerless. For instance, when the British government of India made it a crime to own salt that was not bought from the government, Gandhi led a 200-mile march to the sea. There, he and hundreds of followers made salt from seawater. Martin Luther King (1929–1968) based his code of nonviolence on the teachings of Christianity and on the ideas of Gandhi. He and other African-American leaders of the civil rights movement used sit-ins, demonstrations, marches, and boycotts to end discrimination in housing and the workplace, to work for the enforcement of voting rights, and to make other improvements in the lives of African Americans.

Page 52 Religion has played an important part in the farmworkers' movement. The two largest groups of farmworkers, Mexicans and Filipinos, both hailed from former Spanish colonies that have remained strongly Catholic. It was common for the farmworkers' movement to use elements of Catholic tradition in union activities. Because emphasis on Catholic ritual made some non-Catholic Mexican farmworkers

89

uncomfortable, efforts were later made to incorporate many religious traditions. Doing so was made easier by the fact that clergy from all religious groups eagerly joined *La Causa*. Ironically, many of the growers were also active Catholics. Thus, priests in the grape-growing areas of California often felt divided by the conflict between growers and workers.

Page 55 For the volunteers who traveled across the country to educate people about the boycott, the trip was often a journey into the unknown. Many had never left California before. Now they were given money for bus tickets, the addresses of sympathetic groups, and very little else. When they reached a city after a bus trip of hundreds or even thousands of miles, they were expected to arrange for their own food and lodgings by asking for help from the sympathizers. They were also expected to picket or to give talks in churches, union halls, and school auditoriums to explain the boycott.

Page 60 The pilgrimage (*la peregrinación* in Spanish) is an ancient practice of the Catholic church as well as of Islam, Hinduism, and many other religions. In a pilgrimage, individuals or groups travel to certain locations felt to be holy, such as Jerusalem, Santiago de Compostela in Spain, or the shrine of the Virgin of Guadalupe in Mexico. The purpose of a pilgrimage might be to cleanse one's soul, to demonstrate one's faith, or perhaps to petition God for aid with some problem. It is not coincidental that the march to Sacramento took place during Lent and was timed to end on Easter Sunday, two important events in the Christian religious calendar.

Page 65–67 Robert Kennedy's relationship with Cesar Chavez and the farmworkers' movement continued after the Delano hearings. Kennedy had publicly endorsed many groups who were working for better conditions or for civil rights. In a speech after the hearings, the senator called Chavez "one of the heroic figures of our time." Chavez in turn supported Robert Kennedy in his run for the presidency in 1968. When Kennedy won the California primary in June of 1968, Dolores Huerta was one of the Kennedy supporters at the Ambassador Hotel in Los Angeles. She was in a group of people walking with Kennedy when he was shot to death by an assassin in a passageway of the hotel.

Page 80 When the marchers reached Sacramento, they had hoped to meet with then-governor Edmund "Pat" Brown, a Democrat. Brown, who faced an election that year, decided not to risk offending the powerful growers. Although the lieutenant governor met with the marchers several days before they reached

Sacramento, Governor Brown decided to spend Easter weekend out of town. In November 1966, the Republican candidate Ronald Reagan was elected governor of California, defeating Brown by a landslide. Reagan, however, was even less sympathetic than Brown to the farmworkers.

Dana Catharine de Ruiz is a Spanish teacher and freelance writer. She lives in New York City with her sons, Mario Bernardo and Eduardo Felipe. Ms. Catharine de Ruiz is also the author of *To Fly with the Swallows* for the Stories of America.

Richard Larios is an executive editor at Curriculum Concepts in New York City. He is the supervising editor of the Stories of America. Mr. Larios lives in Bayside, Queens.